NATIONAL GEOGRAPHIC

Ladders

The
Aztec
Pre-Columbian Americans

Moctezuma II

by Erica Lauf

The year is 1502, and the place is Tenochtitlán (tay-nohch-teet-LAHN), the Aztec capital, a bustling city with thriving markets and towering **temples**. On this particular day, a strange excitement crackles in the air. A man, dressed in a regal blue cloak and adorned with jewelry, appears before his people. The man is Moctezuma (mok-tih-ZOO-muh) II—and he has just been crowned the new Aztec emperor, or ruler. This is no small responsibility.

When Moctezuma II came to power, he took control of a vast **empire**. An empire is a group of peoples and states united under one ruler. He expanded the empire farther still and tightened his grasp on the conquered peoples. During his reign, the Aztec Empire was one of the most powerful and advanced civilizations in the world. It stretched across most of present-day central Mexico, from the Atlantic Ocean to the Pacific Ocean. His nearly 20-year reign was marked by wise decisions and deadly missteps, great kindnesses and bloody brutality, glorious victories, and, ultimately, pitiful defeat. Who was Moctezuma II, and how did he become so powerful?

Moctezuma II was the ninth and last ruler of the Aztec Empire. Under the rule of Moctezuma I, the empire had expanded and Tenochtitlán had become the empire's capital city.

From Prince to Power

Today we know Tenochtitlán as Mexico City, the capital of Mexico, but in the late 1400s, it was the heart of the mighty Aztec Empire. Merchants traded goods in lively marketplaces, while great stone temples, such as Templo Mayor, rose skyward, honoring the hundreds of gods and goddesses the Aztec worshipped. Home to hundreds of thousands of people, Tenochtitlán was larger than any European city at that time.

Moctezuma II was born into a family of leaders in about 1467, but becoming emperor was not guaranteed. Moctezuma had many years of schooling and trained hard to become a warrior. Over time, he earned a command in the army.

When Moctezuma was 35, his uncle died and he was chosen to be the new emperor. He soon won respect by rebuilding Tenochtitlán after a disastrous flood. When drought made food scarce, he opened the royal corn silos so his people would have food. But he could be ruthless, too. He demanded goods and materials from conquered towns and took prisoners by the thousands. When towns rebelled, he crushed them. He staged battles just for entertainment, pitting trained warriors against ill-equipped prisoners.

Moctezuma lived a royal lifestyle. People carried him from place to place on a golden litter, or raised platform, so his feet wouldn't touch the ground. He changed clothing four times a day and never wore the same outfit twice! His palace boasted a zoo of exotic animals. But his glory days could not last forever.

∧ Moctezuma won favor with his people by giving them food when they needed it. This drawing from a 1579 Spanish book shows a great Aztec feast.

< Terra-cotta statue of an Eagle Warrior

< While attending warrior school, young Moctezuma mastered the skills and weapons of war. This was necessary training for boys of the ambitious Aztec Empire. Top warriors were called Eagle Warriors. They earned that name by taking at least four captives.

The End of an Empire

In 1519, a new threat emerged, and Moctezuma did not know what to make of it. Reports trickled into the capital city, telling of bizarre visitors along the eastern coast of the empire. These tales described mountains floating on the waves of the sea and pale, bearded men riding deer. In fact, tall ships delivered Spanish **conquistadors** (kahn-KEES-tuh-dawrz), or conquerors, who rode horses, not deer. Hernán Cortés (ur-NAHN kawr-TEHS) was the leader of the conquistadors.

The Aztec had gold, which the conquistadors had heard about and wanted for themselves. The Spaniards had two things the Aztec had never seen before—guns and horses.

Moctezuma did not challenge the Spanish strangers with military force. Instead, he welcomed them to Tenochtitlán with gifts of gold and gems. In the traditions of **Mesoamerica**, an area including present-day Mexico and parts of Central America, a host proved his power and wealth by offering gifts, which is what Moctezuma did. But these gifts just made the Spaniards hungrier for treasure, and they intended to get it.

de los Indios, de Monteçuma, Cortes e S^n Juã d Vl̄ua

Moctezuma met Cortés with gifts. He saw that his warriors were no match for the Spaniards with their guns and horses.

Aztec turquoise serpent

Although Spanish guns astonished and terrified the Aztec, Cortés knew he was outnumbered. Rather than risk a battle, Cortés captured Moctezuma and made him a prisoner in his own palace. With little power left, Moctezuma sat by helplessly as the Spaniards outraged his people. Conquistadors destroyed Aztec religious images, and they killed a disobedient Aztec general. But the final blow came when the Spaniards killed a number of Aztec warriors and noblemen. In a fury, the people rose up in rebellion. Hoping to calm the rioters, the Spaniards led Moctezuma to the palace roof to address his people.

But the Aztec had lost all respect for their leader and began shouting and hurling rocks at him. He died that day, most likely killed by one of those rocks.

Moctezuma died in 1520, less than a year after the Spaniards set foot on Aztec soil. The Aztec Empire crumbled not long after. Cortés and his conquistadors destroyed Tenochtitlán and built their own city on top of it. Today, we know it as Mexico City, the capital of Mexico.

Check In What does the story of Moctezuma's life tell you about what happened to the Aztec Empire?

Foods of the Aztec

by Nathan W. James

What do popcorn, ketchup, and hot chocolate have in common? The Aztec.

Popcorn comes from corn, ketchup comes from tomatoes, and, of course, hot chocolate comes from chocolate. Each of these foods is native to Central and South America, and each was an important part of the Aztec diet. But to the Spaniards and other Europeans of the 1500s, these foods were foreign. The Aztec introduced the Spanish conquistadors to these strange new foods when the Spaniards first arrived in the Aztec Empire. Just think about it. Can you imagine tasting corn, tomatoes, or chocolate for the very first time?

The Spaniards enjoyed these Aztec foods so much that they carried them back across the ocean when they returned home. Once they had introduced these foods to Spain, it didn't take long for all of Europe to become hooked, and corn, tomatoes, and chocolate to become popular foods in Europe. Farmers in Europe began growing tomatoes and corn. European chocolate makers brought in cocoa beans from Mesoamerica and used them to make delicious new treats.

In time, these foods traveled from Europe to North America with European settlers. Today, these foods are included in millions of recipes all over the world. Read on to learn more about how Aztec foods ended up on your plate.

The **Aztec** ate corn, tomatoes, and chocolate.

We know the Aztec ate corn, tomatoes, and chocolate because these foods appear in their art. This modern painting shows the Aztec god of wind giving corn to humans.

Amazing Maize

The Aztec depended on **maize**—or what you might know as corn. Maize was **cultivated**, or planted and grown, in Mesoamerica for thousands of years, and it became a staple in the Aztec diet. The Aztec cooked corn soups and stews, tortillas and tamales, and corn on the cob. They even used the corncobs as fuel for their fires and corn husks to make decorative art and dolls.

> Maize was so important to the Aztec that they held festivals for it during the planting and harvesting seasons. They worshipped a goddess of maize who was often shown carrying ears of corn.

A **maize** goddess!

> This tool is called a metate (muh-TAH-tay). It is a flat stone with a shallow dent in the middle. Metates were essential in Aztec homes. Aztec cooks used them to grind corn into flour. First, they placed pieces of corn, or kernels, on the metate, and then they used another stone to crush the kernels into flour.

The Aztec didn't just eat popcorn. They **wore** it, too!

The Aztec used corn flour to make tortillas (tor-TEE-yuhz). They wrapped beans, meat, or squash in tortillas and dipped them in a spicy chile pepper sauce.

The Aztec weren't the first to pop corn. Many native cultures of the Americas enjoyed this treat, but the Aztec were the first to introduce popcorn to Europeans.

Once the Aztec harvested a fresh ear of corn, they had **many** tasty uses for it.

You Say Tomato
I Say Tomatl

Today, we enjoy tomatoes in many different ways—in sauces and salads, piled on our spaghetti, and dabbed on our fries. The Aztec used tomatoes in many different ways, too. They discovered the tomato by trading with people from South America, where modern scientists believe tomatoes originated. After tasting the South American tomato—*tomatl* (tuh-MAH-tuhl) in the Aztec language—the Aztec began to grow them, too.

The Italians and French called tomatoes **"apples of love"** once they had gotten a taste of them.

> Today, tomatoes are grown and enjoyed all over the world. China, India, Turkey, and the United States are among the largest tomato-growing countries on the globe.

> We can thank the Aztec for tomato ketchup, even if they never made it themselves. In the 1870s, an American food company started making tomato ketchup, and it was an instant hit.

As you can see, tomatoes come in a variety of colors and shapes. There are yellow, green, grape-shaped, and round tomatoes. The round tomatoes are closer to the types the Aztec cultivated and ate.

There are more than **7,500** tomato varieties today.

Tomatoes spread from South America to the Aztec and then to Spain. This farmer in Mexico uses a bucket to harvest tomatoes.

When Hernán Cortés and his crew traveled back to Europe, they carried tomato seeds with them. Soon, tomatoes could be found growing all over Europe, including Italy. Presto! Spaghetti sauce was born.

Without the Aztec, **Italians** might not have started cooking with tomatoes.

Cuckoo for cacao

What's your favorite way of enjoying chocolate? Maybe you like it best in a candy bar, as a tasty drink, or poured over ice cream. If you asked the Aztec to show you how they enjoyed chocolate, they would probably pour you a cup of something similar to hot cocoa. The Aztec called it "drinking chocolate." They believed **cacao** (kuh-KAH-oh) beans used to make chocolate were as valuable as money!

Europeans added sugar and cream to melted chocolate to make it sweeter and tastier. When Europeans came to North America in the 1600s and 1700s, they brought chocolate with them. At first, chocolate was expensive. But in 1894, an American candy maker started the Hershey Chocolate Company. Hershey made large quantities of chocolate bars and other treats in factories. Chocolate then became less expensive and more available to everyone.

The Aztec used **cacao** beans as money!

People in the United States eat more than **650,000 tons** of chocolate each year!

14

> Chocolate comes from a bean inside the fruit of a cacao tree. Other cultures introduced the cacao bean to the Aztec through trade. The Aztec enjoyed the taste of chocolate so much that the beans became very rare—and very valuable. People were soon using cacao beans as money.

< The Aztec served the Spaniards a drink called *xocoatl* (shoh-koh-AHT-uhl), but it was too bitter for them. The Spaniards couldn't pronounce the name, so they called it *chocolate*. This Aztec cup might have been used to serve chocolate. It was carved in the shape of a hare, an animal that looks like a large rabbit.

The Aztec sipped their chocolate drinks through golden straws!

< The Aztec used their metates to grind cacao as well as corn. They mixed the powder with hot water for a yummy chocolate drink.

Spicy Aztec Cocoa

INGREDIENTS

4 cups milk
2 cups light cream
1 1/2 cups semisweet chocolate pieces
1 teaspoon instant coffee
1/8 teaspoon ground chipotle chile pepper
1 teaspoon ground cinnamon, plus extra for sprinkling
whipped cream

DIRECTIONS

1. Combine milk, light cream, chocolate, coffee, ground chipotle, and cinnamon.

2. Place over low heat, stirring constantly until it is just about to boil.

3. Remove from heat and pour into cups. Sprinkle with extra cinnamon, or top with whipped cream if desired.

4. Drink and enjoy!

Check In What kinds of foods do you eat that are made with tomatoes, corn, and chocolate?

15

WELCOME TO TEOTIHUACÁN

by David Holford

∧ Visitors looking out over the ruins of Teotihuacán see the Avenue of the Dead reaching toward the horizon.

We think of the Aztec as a long-gone culture, but wait until you see Teotihuacán (tay-oh-tee-wah-KAHN), an ancient city in present-day Mexico. Hundreds of years before the Aztec ruled this area, Teotihuacán was the home of an ancient civilization and one of the biggest cities in the world. After the Aztec discovered the ruins of the city, Teotihuacán became quite important to them. Today, visitors still flock to Teotihuacán to explore the ruins of this incredible city and to learn a little something about the Aztec, as well as the city's first inhabitants.

Let's stroll down Teotihuacán's main street, the Avenue of the Dead. You're probably wondering who gave this road such a creepy name and why. We have the Aztec to thank for that. When the Aztec first came to Teotihuacán around A.D. 1300, this broad avenue—wider than a 10-lane highway—was lined with low platforms that the Aztec believed to be tombs, or graves. It turns out they were wrong. The platforms were probably the bases of homes left by the ancient people who first lived in the city. Now let's explore some of the amazing buildings along the Avenue of the Dead.

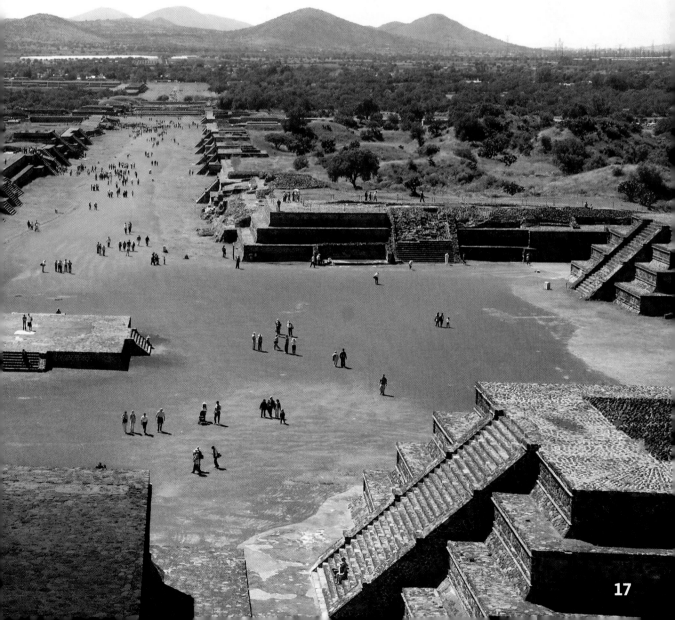

BIRTHPLACE OF THE GODS

Teotihuacán is a city of ruins on top of ruins. Archaeologists do not know what the founders of Teotihuacán called themselves, but they do know these ancient people farmed the countryside in central Mexico beginning around 400 B.C. People in this pre-Aztec civilization built a **sacred**, or holy, city—an important place in their religion. They believed their gods had created the world on that very spot.

Within a century, 200,000 people lived in Teotihuacán. Besides being a center for religion, it was also a center for trade. Merchants from the city traded crafts throughout Mesoamerica. Teotihuacán's culture spread along with its goods.

The city's glory ended around A.D. 750 when enemies burned many buildings to the ground. Residents fled, and over time the city fell into ruin. When the Aztec rediscovered Teotihuacán around 1300, only a hint of its former glory remained. The walls of this ancient city bore pictures of their own gods, so the Aztec named it Teotihuacán, or the "place where the gods were born." The site became sacred to the Aztec as well, and they built their own temples on top of the ruined ones in Teotihuacán.

> This sculpted head of a goddess decorates the Temple of the Feathered Serpent in Teotihuacán.

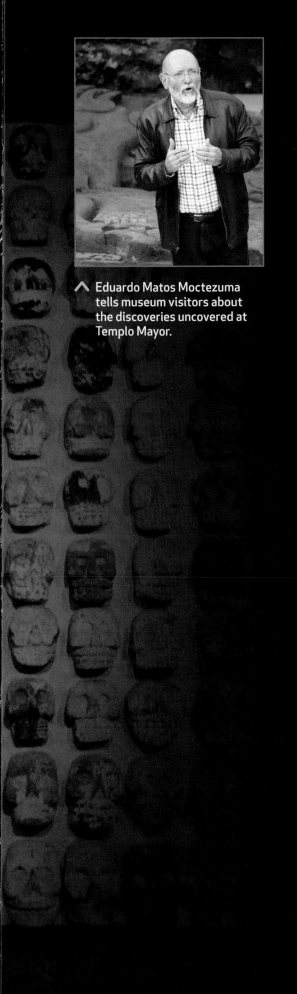

Eduardo Matos Moctezuma tells museum visitors about the discoveries uncovered at Templo Mayor.

Urban archaeologist Eduardo Matos Moctezuma led the scientists who studied the 1978 discovery. Matos Moctezuma and his team already had vast knowledge of the Aztec. But they knew that this discovery was special.

The temple they found was named Templo Mayor (TEM-ploh my-YOR). Matos Moctezuma's team studied the temple and learned that it began as a small structure and grew as Aztec civilization developed.

Matos Moctezuma's team studied the temple over the next few decades. They found new structures and thousands of artifacts. They learned that the temple had been rebuilt seven times. In the temple's final form, two huge 90-foot-tall pyramids stood on its base. One was dedicated to the Aztec god of war. The other was dedicated to the god of rain.

About 6,000 artifacts are displayed at the Templo Mayor museum next to the site. For example, visitors see two life-sized statues of Aztec warriors as well as a wall of skulls from Templo Mayor. At the temple itself, Matos Moctezuma's team has left many artifacts exactly where they stood in the days of the Aztec.

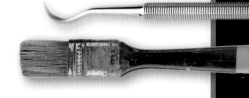

The name Templo Mayor means "Great Temple."

Another Huge Find

Leonardo López Luján is an urban archaeologist who has worked with Eduardo Matos Moctezuma on Templo Mayor since 1980, when López Luján was just 16 years old. This project has been going on for many years, but that doesn't mean the exciting discoveries have slowed down. In 2006, López Luján and his team hit the jackpot. They hauled up a 13-ton rectangular **monolith**, or huge stone column. It was broken into four gigantic pieces. When all the dust was brushed away, they discovered that the stone bore the image of the Aztec goddess of Earth.

The Aztec believed the Earth goddess swallowed the sun every night. Then in the morning, she spit it out again. López Luján learned from historical records that the Aztec used sculptures of the goddess to mark the graves of their dead kings. According to López Luján, the Aztec compared the reign of a king to the sun's path across the sky. A king's reign ended just like the sun ended at sunset—swallowed by the Earth goddess. Then a new king rose in his place.

Today, López Luján and other urban archaeologists continue to search beneath Mexico City for more ruins to dig up and study. As they make new discoveries, they learn more about the great Aztec civilization.

> Workers use straps to move this stone monolith to Templo Mayor museum.

Leonardo López Luján continues to study discoveries at Templo Mayor.

Check In How did city workers help urban archaeologists make a major Aztec discovery?

Aztec Artifacts

by Bryon Cahill

You may have heard the old saying, "A picture is worth a thousand words." Well, the Aztec didn't have a written language, so pictures and art were one way they expressed themselves. The artifacts the Aztec left behind tell us about their culture.

< Aztec artists carved statues of the gods the Aztec so feared and admired. This ceramic vase shows Tlaloc (tuh-LA-lahk), the Aztec god of rain, wearing a turquoise mask.

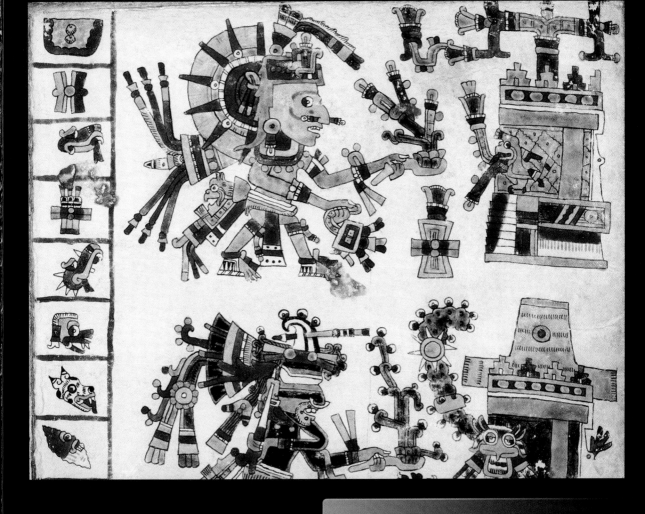

The Aztec created **codices,** or books made up of pictures called **glyphs.** Through the use of glyphs, these books told stories of Aztec culture. This calendar shows offerings being made by the Aztec sun god on the top and the god of darkness on the bottom. The symbols along the left stand for the year the glyphs were written or the year an event happened.

Gold was important to the Aztec. They used it to make everything from figurines of gods to pendants and jewelry. Spanish conquistadors took many of these artifacts back to Europe or melted them down for the valuable gold.

Archaeologists found this gold pendant in the tomb of an Aztec ruler.

Check In What can we learn about the Aztec from the artifacts they left behind?

Discuss

1. What do you think connects the five selections you read in this book? What makes you think that?

2. Describe what happened to the Aztec people when the Spanish arrived in their empire.

3. How did the Aztec foods tomatoes, corn, and chocolate become common around the world?

4. What can we learn about the Aztec by exploring Teotihuacán and Templo Mayor in Mexico City?

5. Which aspect of Aztec history or culture would you like to know more about? Explain.